GRAPHIC LIBRARY

THE LONELY EXISTENCE
OF ASTEROIDS AND COMETS

BY
MARK WEAKLAND

ILLUSTRATED BY
CARLOS AÓN

CAPSTONE PRESS
a capstone imprint

Graphic Library is published by Capstone Press,
1710 Roe Crest Drive, North Mankato, Minnesota 56003.
www.capstonepub.com

 Books published by Capstone Press are manufactured with paper
containing at least 10 percent post-consumer waste.

Library of Congress Cataloging-in-Publication Data
Weakland, Mark.
  The lonely existence of asteroids and comets / by Mark Weakland.
    p. cm.—(Graphic library. Adventures in science)
  Includes bibliographical references and index.
  Summary: "In graphic novel format, explores asteroids and comets, including their
formation, differences, and impact on life on Earth"—Provided by publisher.
  ISBN 978-1-4296-7546-8 (library binding)
  ISBN 978-1-4296-7987-9 (paperback)
  1. Asteroids—Juvenile literature. 2. Comets—Juvenile literature. I. Title.
  QB651.W396 2012
  523.44—dc23   2011033563

Art Director
Nathan Gassman

Designer
Lori Bye

Editor
Anthony Wacholtz

Production Specialist
Laura Manthe

Colorist
Laura Lazzati

Consultant:
Leslie F. Bleamaster III
Research Scientist
Planetary Science Institute
Tucson, Arizona

Printed in the United States of America in Stevens Point, Wisconsin.
102011   006404WZS12

TABLE OF CONTENTS

CHAPTER 1

A LONELY EXISTENCE

People aren't often alone. We gather in villages, towns, and cities. We join together for meetings, reunions, or just to chat. That's not the case with comets and asteroids. They live lonely lives.

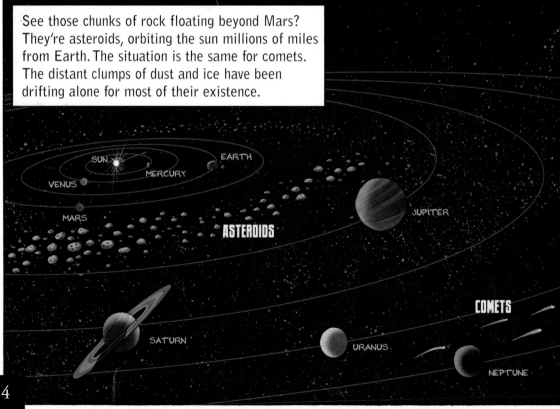

See those chunks of rock floating beyond Mars? They're asteroids, orbiting the sun millions of miles from Earth. The situation is the same for comets. The distant clumps of dust and ice have been drifting alone for most of their existence.

SUN

EARTH

MERCURY

VENUS

MARS

ASTEROIDS

JUPITER

COMETS

SATURN

URANUS

NEPTUNE

Every now and then, comets fly by Earth close enough to be seen with the naked eye. As a comet travels toward the sun, it leaves behind a huge plume of dust and rock.

Sometimes comets and asteroids get too close for comfort. A piece of an asteroid may pass through Earth's atmosphere as a meteor. If it survives its fiery fall to Earth, it's called a meteorite.

Luckily, most comets and asteroids never get near Earth. We learn about them as we peer through telescopes and receive spacecraft signals. Although they're fascinating, life is safer when comets and asteroids keep their distance.

CHAPTER 2

HOME SWEET SOLAR SYSTEM

Look up on a clear, dark night and you'll see a bright, misty band of stars spreading across the sky. That's the center of our galaxy, the Milky Way.

With its planets, comets, and asteroids, our solar system is a tiny part of the Milky Way. To understand how the solar system came to be, let's travel back five billion years when there was no solar system. Instead, giant stars blazed within gigantic clouds of gas and dust.

Occasionally a super giant star would explode. The explosion, called a supernova, probably started the formation of our solar system. Shock waves from the explosion pushed together the cloud's gas and dust. Gravity then began pulling the gas and dust into clumps.

Over time a huge rotating disk took shape. As the disk turned, dust clumped together and became rocks. The rocks broke apart and smashed back together. The process repeated over and over again for millions of years. The clumps and rocks grew to enormous sizes.

At some point, a very large mass in the center of the disk ignited and the sun was born. Other clumps formed the eight main planets and the dwarf planets Ceres, Pluto, and Eris.

Asteroids and comets formed from the same material that made the planets. Asteroids are mostly rock and metal. They formed closer to the sun. Comets are made up of ice, dust, and organic materials. They formed much farther from the sun.

In the early days of the solar system, trillions of asteroids and comets whizzed through space. They crashed into the planets and each other. Eventually, they settled in places far from Earth.

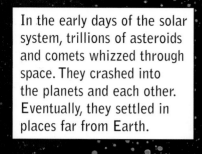

One group of comets now makes up the Kuiper belt. The Kuiper belt encircles the solar system. Starting at Neptune's orbit, the belt extends billions of miles into space.

OORT CLOUD

200 TRILLION MILES FROM EARTH

KUIPER BELT

OUR SOLAR SYSTEM

Another group of comets gathers farther out in the Oort cloud. Found more than 200 trillion miles (322 trillion kilometers) from Earth, the Oort cloud completely surrounds our solar system.

Most asteroids are located within the asteroid belt. This belt of rocky debris lies between Mars and Jupiter. The asteroids range in size from small boulders to mountains. There may be millions of asteroids within the asteroid belt.

SUN
MERCURY
VENUS
EARTH
MARS
JUPITER

FACT
More than 300,000 asteroids have been found by astronomers. Of these, at least 26 are larger than 124 miles (200 km) wide.

Some asteroids are so large they have names, such as Vesta, Pallas, and Hygiea. Ceres, named after the Roman goddess of grain, is so large that it's considered a dwarf planet. Its length would almost stretch across the state of Montana.

9

Asteroids can be put into three groups: stony, iron-nickel, and a mixture of the two. Of all the known asteroids, only a small number are iron-nickel.

Iron-nickel asteroids are mostly metal. In addition to iron and nickel, they contain platinum, cobalt, and manganese. They also contain minerals such as sulfur.

MINING ASTEROIDS

Once all the metal on Earth is mined, where will future supplies come from? Asteroids! Even a small iron-nickel asteroid can contain 30 billion tons (27 billion metric tons) of rock and metal ore. It would take 100 NASA space shuttles 6 million trips each to move half of an asteroid's ore to Earth!

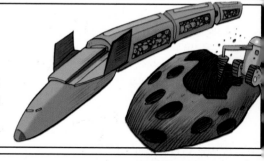

Unlike asteroids, the rock in a comet is mostly dust, tiny grains of sand, and ice. Most of the ice is made of water, but some is made of carbon dioxide. Carbon dioxide ice is also known as dry ice.

There's also organic material in comets. It looks like coal dust or soot from a fire. Where did the sooty organic material come from? It came from the large clouds that formed long before our solar system.

DUST

DRY ICE

SAND GRAINS

WATER ICE

FACT The *Giotto* space probe snapped a picture of a comet's main body, called the nucleus. The comet's nucleus was 9 miles (14 km) long, black, and shaped like a peanut.

After making several trips around the sun, a comet's ice forms a crust of rock, dust, and organic material. Comets are some of the darkest objects in the solar system. The black asphalt of a parking lot reflects more light than a deep-space comet.

Comets aren't always dark and difficult to see. When a comet nears the sun, ice and dust stream off of its nucleus to form a coma and tail.

The tail of dust particles and ice reflects light from the sun. Comet tails range in length from tens of thousands to millions of miles long!

As Earth moves through a comet's plume, particles of dust and rock burn up in the atmosphere. These bits of blazing dust and rock are known as meteors.

During the Great Meteor Shower of 1835, "shooting stars" fell at the rate of hundreds of thousands an hour! The shower was caused by Earth colliding with the densest part of a comet's trail of debris.

Within the asteroid belt, asteroids often collide. When one hits another, chunks break off. During really big collisions, entire asteroids shatter into smaller pieces. If the orbits of the pieces cross Earth's orbit, look out for a collision!

Meteorites have shown up all over the world. More than 100 large impact craters have been found.

Impact craters form when a meteorite strikes Earth with great force. The largest one ever found is about 186 miles (300 km) across.

WHAT MAKES UP A METEORITE?

A chunk of rock that hits Earth is known as a meteorite. Usually these rocks aren't from comets, though. Meteorites are chunks of stone or iron and nickel that have broken off of asteroids.

CHAPTER 3

COMET TALES

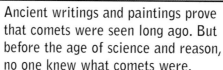

Ancient writings and paintings prove that comets were seen long ago. But before the age of science and reason, no one knew what comets were.

Early stargazers were startled when they saw lights where none had been before. Were the lights angels? Could they be warning signs from an angry god?

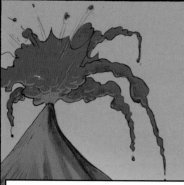

Ancient people believed comets were bearers of bad news. When a comet appeared, most people thought a war, disease, or natural disaster was sure to follow.

FACT
The word "disaster" has its roots in the ancient belief that comets brought bad news. Disaster is Greek for "bad star."

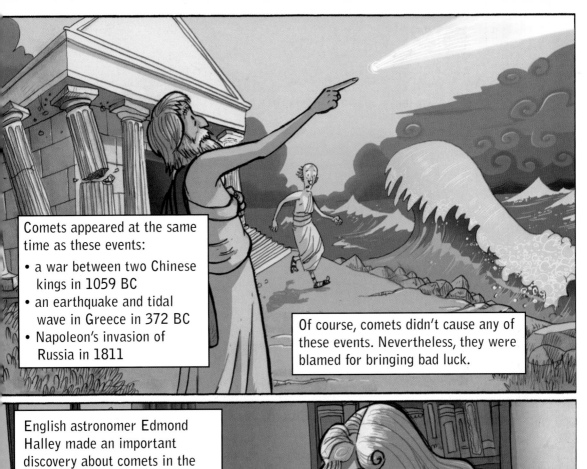

Comets appeared at the same time as these events:

- a war between two Chinese kings in 1059 BC
- an earthquake and tidal wave in Greece in 372 BC
- Napoleon's invasion of Russia in 1811

Of course, comets didn't cause any of these events. Nevertheless, they were blamed for bringing bad luck.

English astronomer Edmond Halley made an important discovery about comets in the early 1700s. He discovered comets that appeared in different centuries were actually the same comet showing up over and over again.

Halley knew that the planets orbited the sun along oval-shaped paths called ellipses. He thought comets might do the same. He believed comets loop around the sun on a regular basis called a period.

Later in life, Halley thought about the comets that appeared in 1531, 1607, and 1682. Halley guessed the three comets were actually just one. He predicted the comet would reappear in December of 1758.

Although Halley didn't live to see it, his prediction was right! A comet blazed brightly in the sky on December 25, 1758.

Since Halley's death, historians and astronomers have looked over ancient manuscripts that mention comets. We now know that Halley's comet has made at least 28 visits to Earth, reappearing once every 76 years.

Halley's comet will be making an appearance again in 2061. How old will you be when the famous comet appears again?

Because comets orbit the sun, they regularly visit Earth. But because of their long orbits, regular may not mean frequent. Comet Hale-Bopp, which amazed sky watchers in 1997, last visited the Earth around 2400 BC!

CHAPTER 4

CRASH LANDING

Long ago Earth was bombarded by comets large and small. The colliding comets supplied Earth with materials needed for life, including carbon and water.

During the first 500 millions years of its existence, Earth had little oxygen, water, or organic material. Without these substances, there was only a small chance that life would develop.

In 1986 the *Giotto* space probe flew through the tail of Halley's comet. The probe analyzed the material streaming from the comet's nucleus and coma.

The comet was 80 percent water. It also contained carbon monoxide, methane, and ammonia. All of these compounds are common on Earth.

Eighteen years after *Giotto*, NASA's *Stardust* spacecraft chased down the comet Wild 2 (pronounced Vilt 2). *Stardust*'s job was to collect tiny particles from the comet's tail. In the wispy threads of comet dust, the spacecraft found traces of glycine, an organic compound. Without glycine, life on Earth could not exist.

Some scientists think that the building blocks of life first formed in outer space. *Stardust*'s discovery supports this belief. Life-creating molecules were carried from space to Earth by crashing comets. Perhaps comets carried these same molecules to other planets too. If these organic molecules exist on other planets, life may exist elsewhere in the galaxy.

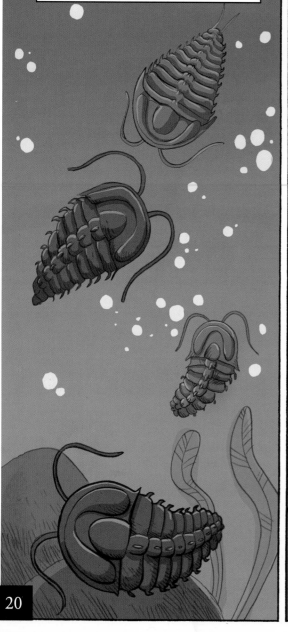

Comets crashed to Earth over a long time period. But the collisions happened less often over time. Earth's surface became stable and life took hold.

Oceans formed and aquatic plants grew. After hundreds of millions of years, strange creatures evolved and swam through the warm seas.

More time passed and dinosaurs came to rule Earth. For tens of millions of years, they slithered, swam, and stomped across the face of the planet. Then, suddenly, they were gone.

Why did dinosaurs die out so quickly? Recent discoveries pin the blame on a massive comet or asteroid strike.

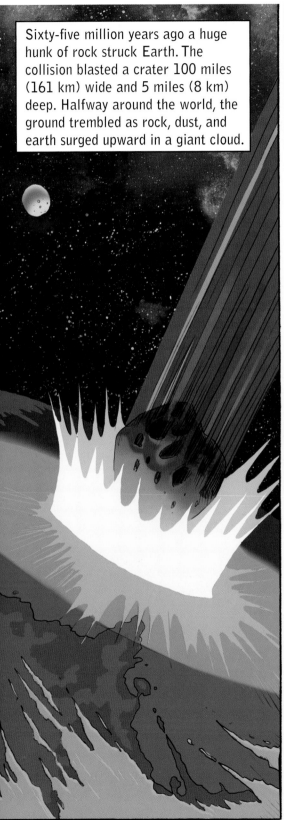

Sixty-five million years ago a huge hunk of rock struck Earth. The collision blasted a crater 100 miles (161 km) wide and 5 miles (8 km) deep. Halfway around the world, the ground trembled as rock, dust, and earth surged upward in a giant cloud.

The shock wave from the explosion forced the seas into a tsunami thousands of feet high. Meanwhile, hurricane force winds carrying rock and dust shredded everything in its path. The intense heat of the impact ignited fires across the planet. Smoke filled the air, making breathing difficult for any animals left alive.

The comet collision doomed the dinosaurs. Many died quickly. A thick cloud of dust blotted out the sun for months or possibly years. Plants died from lack of sunlight, so plant-eating dinosaurs didn't have much food. Water froze, even at the equator.

Dinosaur extinction, however, was good news for the smaller creatures that survived. With dinosaurs no longer around, small rodents were less likely to be eaten.

As millions of years passed, the small mammals that survived slowly evolved into larger ones. Some took to the trees and became ape-like primates. Millions of years later they came down from the trees and began to walk upright.

While the great collision 65 million years ago brought death to the dinosaurs, it allowed our ancestors to survive and thrive. If it wasn't for the collision, humans might not be here today.

If you look up at the night sky, you might see a shooting star. These meteors streak through the sky on a regular basis.

Small meteorites hit Earth every few decades. A bigger object might strike once every 100,000 years. Only once every 100 million years does our planet get clobbered by a rock big enough to destroy life on a large scale.

Comets colliding with planets aren't just ancient history. In 1994 the world watched as fragments of the comet Shoemaker-Levy plowed into Jupiter.

At least 21 chunks slammed into the planet's atmosphere at speeds of about 129,000 miles (207,605 km) per hour. The largest fragments tore a hole in the cloud layer big enough to hold two Earths.

Needless to say, scientists—and everyone else—hope a collision won't happen anytime soon. Space agencies are working to prevent a future strike. They track comets, asteroids, and meteors. They figure out whether any will collide with Earth.

Another option would be to crash a very large spacecraft into the asteroid. The force of the nudge might be strong enough to push it away from its collision course.

What if astronomers knew an asteroid would hit Earth in several years? With ample warning, we could nudge an asteroid away from a collision course. For a forceful nudge, nuclear bombs could explode next to the asteroid. The explosion would be close enough to shift the asteroid off course but not close enough to shatter it.

An asteroid could also be gently nudged by powerful spacecraft that have landed on its surface. Constantly running the spacecrafts' engines would provide a steady force to move the asteroid a few inches every year. As the years passed, the asteroid would be inched into an orbit that would miss Earth.

If a tracking system discovered a comet or asteroid heading directly for Earth, timing would be crucial. Without enough warning, a powerful nuclear bomb might only shatter an asteroid into chunks. And being pummeled by chunks might be worse than being struck by one large rock.

WONDERS NEVER CEASE

Comets and asteroids exist far from Earth. Even so, we know a lot about them. They formed billions of years ago from the same substances that make up our own planet. Asteroids are rocky and sometimes made of iron and nickel. Comets are made up of dust, organic compounds, and ice.

The solar system is a place of tremendous energy and action. Comets gather speed as they approach the sun. Asteroids tumble and occasionally collide in the asteroid belt beyond Mars.

Sometimes asteroids and comets visit Earth. As comets fly by, their brilliant plumes of water and dust spread across the sky. Asteroid chunks collide with Earth's atmosphere, burning up in streaks of fire.

In your lifetime, a chunk of space rock may fall to Earth. If you're lucky, you might see Halley's comet. It's even possible that you'll watch live video of astronauts walking across the surface of a far off asteroid. In a universe as grand as ours, the wonders never cease.

GLOSSARY

aquatic (uh-KWAH-tik)—describes a plant or animal that lives in water

atmosphere (AT-muhss-fihr)—the mixture of gases that surrounds Earth

coma (KOH-muh)—the temporary area around a comet's nucleus that is composed of gas and small solid particles

debris (duh-BREE)—the scattered pieces of something that has been broken or destroyed

ellipse (i-LIPS)—a shape similar to an oval

galaxy (GAL-uhk-see)—a very large group of stars and planets

gravity (GRAV-uh-tee)—a force that pulls objects with mass together; gravity pulls objects down toward the center of Earth

ignite (ig-NITE)—to set fire to something

meteor (MEE-tee-ur)—a piece of rock or dust that enters Earth's atmosphere, causing a streak of light in the sky

meteorite (MEE-tee-ur-rite)—a meteoroid that lands on Earth's surface

molecule (MOL-uh-kyool)—the smallest unit of a substance that can exist; a molecule is made of one or more atoms

nucleus (NOO-klee-uhss)—the main body of a comet

orbit (OR-bit)—the path that a celestial body follows; a single revolution of one body around another

organic (or-GAN-ik)—to do with or coming from living things

plume (PLOOM)—an area of dust and rock following a comet

solar system (SOH-lur SISS-tuhm)—the sun and the objects that move around it

supernova (soo-pur-NOH-vuh)—an explosion of a very large star

tail (TAYL)—the part of a comet composed of small particles of dust and ice from the nucleus

READ MORE

Aguilar, David A. *13 Planets: The Latest View of the Solar System.* Washington, D.C.: National Geographic, 2011.

Benson, Michael. *Beyond: A Solar System Voyage.* New York: Abrams Books for Young Readers, 2009.

Carson, Mary Kay. *Far-Out Guide to Asteroids and Comets.* Far-Out Guide to the Solar System. Berkeley Heights, N.J.: Bailey Books, 2011.

Kortenkamp, Steve. *Asteroids, Comets, and Meteoroids.* The Solar System and Beyond. Mankato, Minn.: Capstone Press, 2012.

INTERNET SITES

FactHound offers a safe, fun way to find Internet sites related to this book. All of the sites on FactHound have been researched by our staff.

Here's all you do:

Visit www.facthound.com

Type in this code: 9781429675468

Check out projects, games and lots more at
www.capstonekids.com

INDEX